V&A Pattern
Kimono

V&A Publishing

V&A Pattern
Kimono

First published by V&A Publishing, 2010
V&A Publishing
Victoria and Albert Museum
South Kensington
London SW7 2RL

ISBN 978 1 85177 606 1
Library of Congress Control Number 2009932467

10 9 8 7 6 5 4 3 2 1
2014 2013 2012 2011 2010

A catalogue record for this book is available
from the British Library.

Design: Rose

Front cover (A):
Kimono, crêpe silk with freehand paste-resist and embroidered decoration
Japan, 1900–20 (V&A: FE.233–1974 Hardcastle Gift)
Pages 2–3 (B):
Kimono, monochrome figured satin silk with freehand paste-resist
and embroidered decoration
Japan, 1860–90 (V&A: 874–1891)
Page 6 (C):
Kimono fabric sample, crêpe silk with printed decoration
Japan, 1939 (V&A: FE.22–1997)
Page 11 (D):
Outer kimono, satin silk with embroidered decoration
Japan, 1820–60 (V&A: FE.11–1983)
Pages 78–9 (E):
Kimono, crêpe silk with freehand paste-resist, stencilled and embroidered decoration
Japan, 1780–1830 (V&A: FE.12–1983)

Letters (in brackets) refer to the file name of the
images on the accompanying disc.

Printed in China

V&A Publishing
Victoria and Albert Museum
South Kensington
London SW7 2RL
www.vandabooks.com

V&A Pattern

Each *V&A Pattern* book is an introduction to the Victoria and Albert Museum's extraordinarily diverse collection. The museum has more than three million designs for textiles, decorations, wallpapers and prints; some well-known, others less so. This series explores pattern-making in all its forms, across the world and through the centuries. The books are intended to be both beautiful and useful – showing patterns to enjoy in their own right and as inspiration for new design.

V&A Pattern presents the greatest names and styles in design, while also highlighting the work of anonymous draughtsmen and designers, often working unacknowledged in workshops, studios and factories, and responsible for designs of aesthetic originality and technical virtuosity. Many of the most interesting and imaginative designs are seen too rarely. *V&A Pattern* gathers details from our best objects and hidden treasures from pattern books, swatch books, company archives, design records and catalogues to form a fascinating introduction to the variety and beauty of pattern at the V&A.

The compact disc at the back of each book invites you to appreciate the ingenuity of the designs, and the endless possibilities for their application. To use the images professionally, you need permission from V&A Images, as the V&A controls – on behalf of others – the rights held in its books and CD-Roms. *V&A Pattern* can only ever be a tiny selection of the designs available at www.vandaimages.com. We see requests to use images as an opportunity to help us to develop and improve our licensing programme – and for us to let you know about images you may not have found elsewhere.

Kimono Patterns
Anna Jackson

Japan has a very rich textile history, the major focus of interest and artistic expression being the kimono, which from the sixteenth century was the principal item of dress for all classes and both sexes. Kimono are straight-seamed garments worn wrapped left side over right and secured with a sash called an *obi*. It is not the cut of the garment but the pattern on the surface that is significant with indications of gender, age, social status, personal identity and cultural sensitivity being expressed through colour and decoration.

In the sixteenth century there were no substantial differences between the kimono worn by men and women, but distinctions became more pronounced in the course of the seventeenth century. The patterns on women's kimono became larger and bolder with younger women's kimono being particularly lavishly decorated and brightly coloured. In early kimono the surface was divided into irregular pattern areas. Over time such compartmentalization gave way to an approach which considered the garment as a whole, and in which technique and motif, pattern and ground were fully integrated. With the taste for dynamic, unified motifs, the clean, straight lines of the T-shaped garment served as a blank canvas, or scroll, for the kimono designer.

The images used on kimono often have complex levels of meaning, and many have specific auspicious significance which derives from religious or popular beliefs. The crane for example, is believed to live for a thousand years and to inhabit the land of the immortals and is thus a symbol of longevity and good fortune. The use of specific motifs can allude to the virtues or attributes of the wearer (or those they might aspire to), reflect particular emotions, or relate to the season or occasion. Such symbolism was used especially on kimono worn for celebratory events such as weddings and festivals, when it served to bestow good fortune on the wearer, wrapping them in divine benevolence and protection. Paired ducks, for example, are a symbol of conjugal harmony.

Colours too have strong metaphorical and cultural connotations. Dyes are seen to embody the spirit of the plants from which they are extracted. Any medicinal property is also believed to be transferred to the coloured cloth. Blue derives from indigo (*ai*), which is used to treat bites and stings, so wearing blue fabric serves as a repellent to snakes and insects. Colours also have strong poetic significance. Perhaps the most popular colour for kimono is red, derived from safflower (*benibana*). Red connotes youthful glamour and allure, and is therefore suitable for the garments of young women. It is also a symbol of passionate but – as beni-red easily fades – transient love.

Nature provides the richest source for kimono motifs. Numerous flowers such as peonies, wisteria, bush clover and hollyhocks appear on garments. Many of them, such as cherry blossom, chrysanthemums and maple leaves, have a seasonal significance. Pine, bamboo and plum are known collectively as the 'Three Friends of Winter' (*shōchikubai*), and are symbols of longevity, perseverance and renewal. Birds, animals, butterflies and dragonflies also appear on kimono, along with other motifs drawn from the natural world such as water, snow and clouds. On some kimono whole landscapes of mountains and streams are depicted. Individual natural elements that appear on kimono usually have strong poetic associations, while more complex landscape scenes often refer to particular stories drawn either from classical literature or popular myths. While carrying an auspicious meaning, such motifs also served to demonstrate the literary discernment and cultural sensitivities of the wearer. Although these stories invariably involved people, it is relatively unusual to find human figures depicted on kimono. Instead there are objects that suggest their presence or recent departure, a pair of dropped fans, for example, alluding to lovers disturbed.

In the late nineteenth century Japan underwent a major transformation and modernization with the textile industry being one of the first to adopt western science and technology. Chemical dyes allowed for the creation of dazzling colours, while the development of new types of silk and innovative patterning techniques made relatively inexpensive, highly fashionable garments available to more people than ever before. The range of patterns also widened as western motifs became popular. These trends continued in the early twentieth century. Although western-style clothes gained popularity among women, the kimono continued to be worn. The traditional cut of the garment remained the same, but the motifs were dramatically enlarged and new designs appeared, inspired by western styles such as Art Nouveau and Art Deco. The increasing use of graphic imagery was also seen on kimono for young boys where motifs such as cars, trains and aeroplanes were used as symbols of Japan's modernity.

Since the end of the Second World War western-style clothing has been the everyday wear of most Japanese. Although the kimono is worn much less, it remains an enduring symbol of Japanese culture. Most contemporary textile designers working with traditional techniques still use the kimono as the primary format for their artistic expression, creating highly modern designs that are often still inspired by natural forms and classical literature.

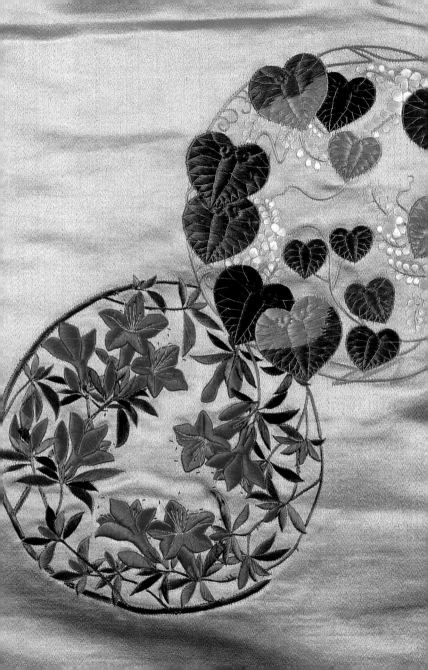

1
Kimono fabric sample, plain weave cotton
Tamba district, Japan, 1800–1900 (V&A: T.100Q–1969)

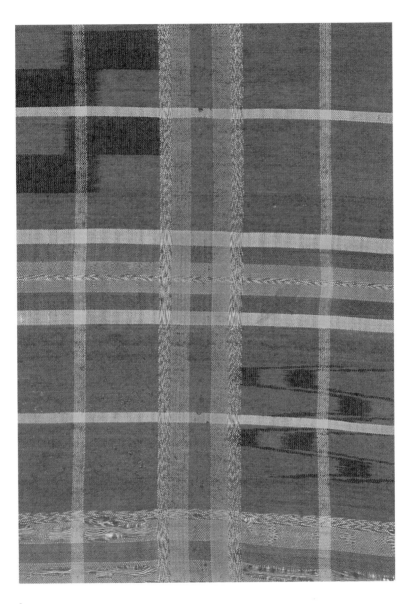

2
Kimono fabric sample, plain weave silk woven with selectively pre-dyed yarns
Okinawa, Rūkyū Islands, 1800–1900 (V&A: T.142–1968)

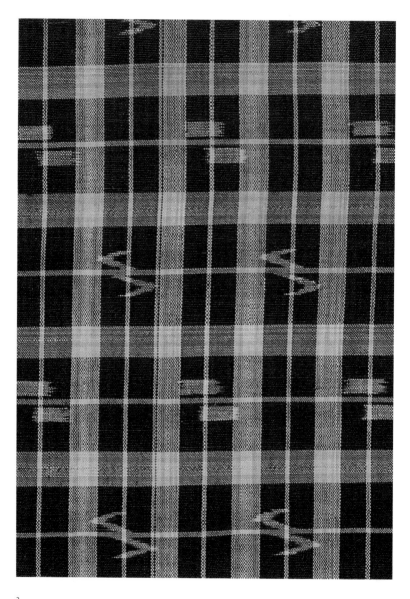

3
Kimono fabric sample, plain weave cotton woven with selectively pre-dyed yarns
Okinawa, Ryūkyū Islands, 1800–1900 (V&A: T.110–1957)

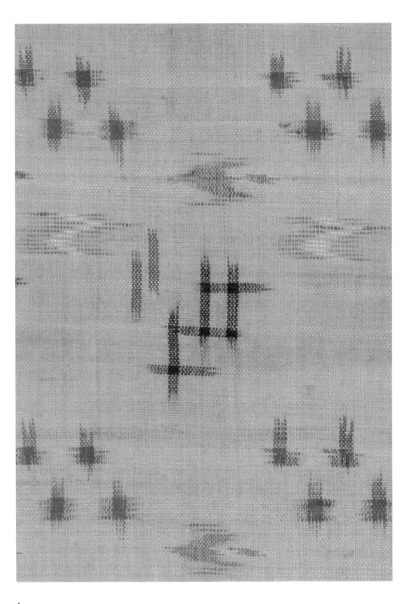

4
Kimono fabric sample, plain weave silk woven with selectively pre-dyed yarns
Okinawa, Ryūkyū Islands, 1800–1900 (V&A:T.142–1968)

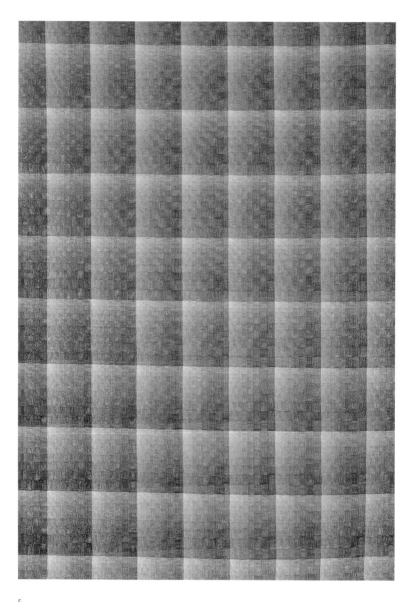

5
Tsuchiya Yoshinori, kimono entitled *Blue Mountains and Green Rivers*
Plain weave and gauze weave figured silk. Gifu Prefecture, Japan, 2004–6 (V&A: 144–2006)

6
Shimura Fukumi, kimono entitled *Ise*
Plain weave silk. Kyoto, Japan, 1988 (V&A: FE.11–1989)

7
Kimono, plain weave banana fibre with stencilled decoration
Okinawa, Ryūkyū Islands, 1880–1920 (V&A: FE.7–1983)

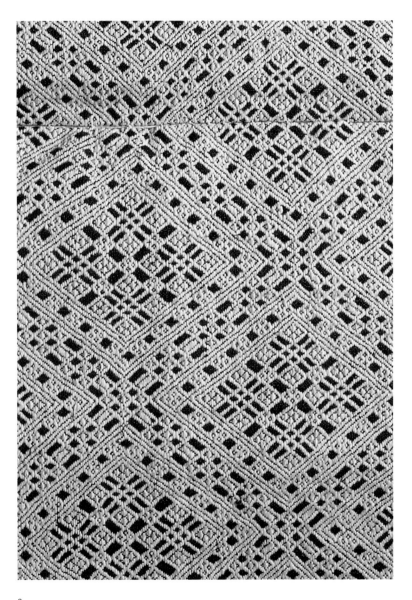

8
Kimono, plain weave bast fibre with embroidered decoration
Tsugara district, Japan, 1890–1930 (V&A: FE.141–1983)

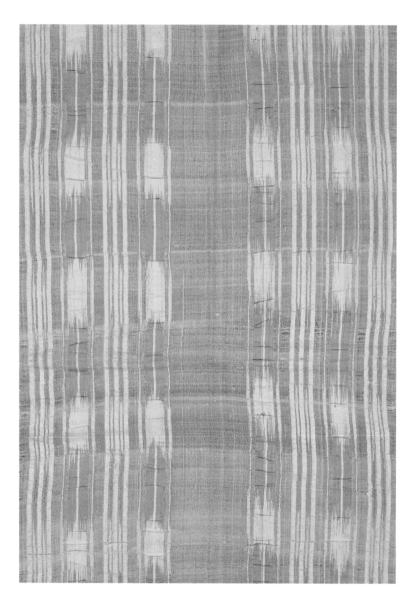

9
Length of kimono fabric, plain weave silk woven with selectively pre-dyed yarns
Japan, 1860–74 (V&A: AP.43:6–1876)

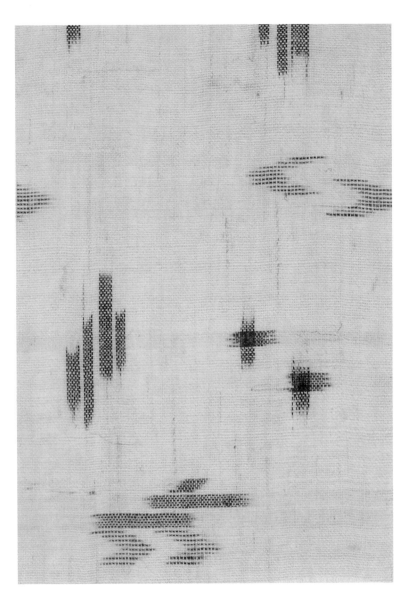

10
Kimono fabric sample, plain weave bast fibre woven with selectively pre-dyed yarns
Okinawa, Ryūkyū Islands, 1800–1900 (V&A: T.142–1968)

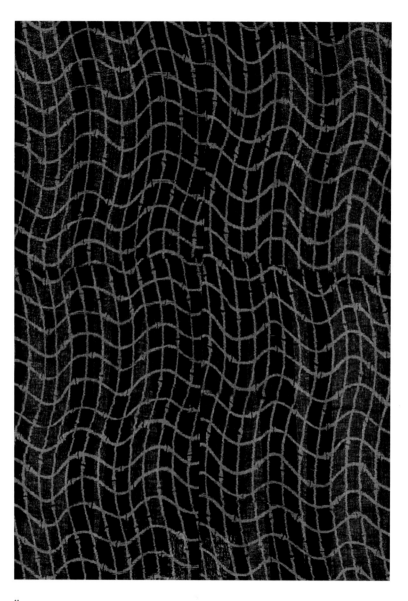

11
Kimono, plain weave bast fibre woven with selectively pre-dyed yarns
Japan, 1920–40 (V&A: FE.316–2005)

12
Moriguchi Kunihiko, kimono entitled *Grey of Dawn*
Plain weave silk with freehand paste-resist decoration. Kyoto, Japan, 1987 (V&A: FE.421–1992)

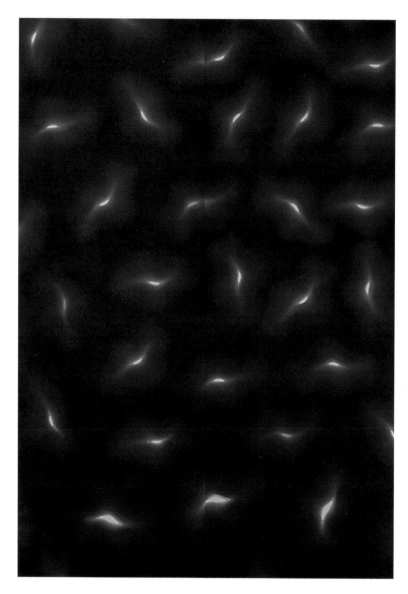

13
Matsubara Yoshichi, kimono entitled *Flight*
Crêpe silk with stencilled decoration. Tokyo, Japan, 1990 (V&A: FE.10−1995)

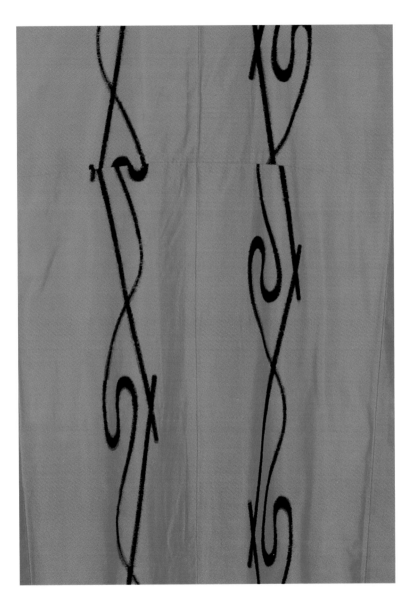

14
Kimono, plain weave silk woven with stencil-printed warp and weft threads
Japan, 1920–40 (V&A: FE.142–2002, Given by Moe Co. Ltd)

15
Moriguchi Kunihiko, kimono entitled *Green Waves*
Plain weave silk with freehand paste-resist decoration. Kyoto, Japan, 1973 (V&A: FE.420–1992)

16
Kimono, stencil-printed gauze weave silk
Japan, 1930–39 (V&A: FE.146–2002, Given by Moe Co. Ltd)

17
Length of kimono fabric, plain weave bast fibre woven with selectively pre-dyed yarns
Japan, 1860–1900 (V&A: T.99–1957)

18
Kimono, polychrome figured silk
Japan, 1860–80 (V&A: T.65–1915, Given by T.B. Clark-Thornhill)

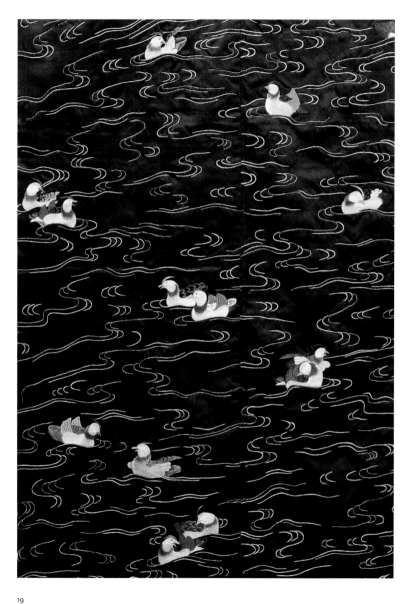

19
Kimono, satin silk with embroidered decoration
Japan, 1820–60 (V&A: FE.28–1987)

20
Kimono, satin silk with embroidered decoration
Japan, 1820–60 (V&A: T.79–1927, Given by T.B. Clark-Thornhill)

21
Child's kimono, plain weave bast fibre with stencilled decoration
Okinawa, Ryūkyū Islands, 1870–1910 (V&A: T.19–1963)

22
Kimono, plain weave bast fibre with freehand paste-resist, stencilled and embroidered decoration
Japan, 1800–50 (V&A: T.87–1968, G. Saumarez Gift)

23
Length of kimono fabric, monochrome figured satin silk with applied gold leaf, tie-dyed and embroidered decoration
Japan, 1600–50 (V&A: 1588–1899)

24
Kimono, satin silk with embroidered decoration
Japan, 1880–1900 (V&A:T.178–1967)

25
Kimono, crêpe silk with printed decoration
Japan, 1960–1980 (V&A: FE.149–2002, Given by Moe Co. Ltd)

26
Length of kimono fabric, monochrome figured satin silk with freehand paste-resist and embroidered decoration
Japan, 1800–60 (V&A: 79–1884)

27
Length of kimono fabric, crêpe silk with freehand paste-resist decoration
Japan, 1890–1912 (V&A: T.429–1912, Strange Gift)

28
Length of kimono fabric, crêpe silk with freehand paste-resist decoration
Japan, 1860–67 (V&A: 842–1869)

29
Kimono fabric sample, gauze weave silk with freehand paste-resist decoration
Japan, 1860–80 (V&A:T.50–1935, Gilbertson Gift)

30
Length of kimono fabric, plain weave bast fibre with freehand paste-resist decoration
Japan, 1820–80 (V&A: T.137–1968)

31
Kimono, plain weave bast fibre with freehand paste-resist and tie-dyed decoration
Japan, 1820–80 (V&A: T.17–1963)

32
Furusawa Machiko, kimono entitled *Myriad Green Leaves*
Figured silk with tie-dyed and painted decoration. Ōita prefecture, Japan, 1992 (V&A: FE.422–1992)

33
Kimono, monochrome figured satin silk with stencilled and embroidered decoration
Japan, 1750–1800 (V&A: FE.8–1987)

34
Kimono, crêpe silk with tie-dyed, freehand paste-resist and embroidered decoration
Japan, 1800–50 (V&A: T.109–1954, Hart Gift)

35
Kimono, silk crêpe woven with supplementary wefts of silver
Japan, 1900–50 (V&A: FE.1–2008, Presented by Philomena Guillebaud through The Art Fund)

36
Kimono, monochrome figured silk with tie-dyed, stencilled and embroidered decoration
Japan, 1700–50 (V&A: FE.13–1983)

37
Kimono, plain weave bast fibre woven with selectively pre-dyed yarns
Japan, 1850–1900 (V&A: T.329–1960)

38
Robe, plain weave cotton with stencilled decoration
Okinawa, Ryūkyū Islands, 1800–70 (V&A: T.295–1960)

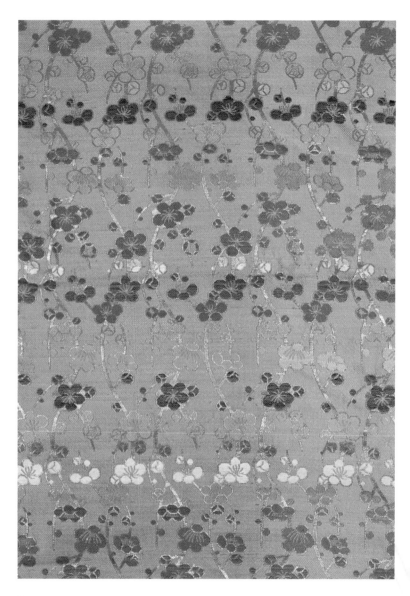

39
Outer kimono (see also plate 40), polychrome figured silk
Japan, 1850–80 (V&A: T.78–1927, Given by T.B. Clark-Thornhill)

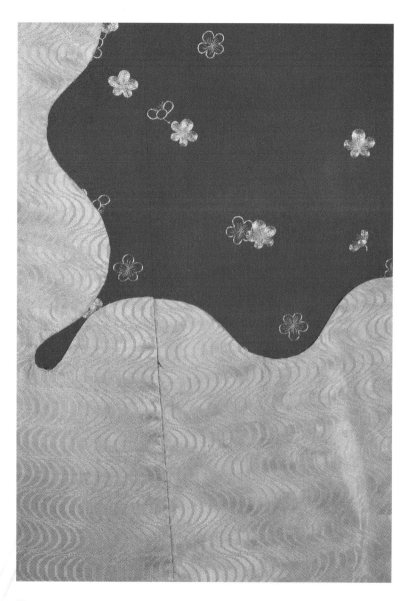

40
Lining of outer kimono (see also plate 39), monochrome figured twill silk and crêpe silk with embroidered decoration
Japan, 1850–80 (V&A: T.78–1927, Given by T.B. Clark-Thornhill)

41
Kimono fabric sample, plain weave silk or synthetic fibre with printed decoration
Japan, 1938 (V&A: FE.18–1997)

42
Kimono, monochrome figured satin silk with freehand paste-resist, stencilled and applied gold leaf decoration
Japan, 1940–60 (V&A: FE.67–1997, Navaro Gift)

43
Kimono, crêpe silk with stencil-printed warp and weft threads
Japan, 1930–50 (V&A: FE.162–1988)

44
Kimono jacket, figured crêpe silk with printed decoration
Japan, 1920–30 (V&A: FE.163–1988)

45
Kimono, plain weave silk woven with stencil-printed warp threads
Japan, 1910–30 (V&A: FE.144–2002, Given by Moe Co. Ltd)

46
Under kimono, figured twill silk with printed decoration
Japan, 1940–50 (V&A: FE.14–1987)

47
Kimono, monochrome figured satin silk with stencilled, painted and embroidered decoration
Japan, 1780–1800 (V&A: FE.106–1982)

48
Kimono, monochrome figured satin silk with tie-dyed decoration
Japan, 1790–1830 (V&A: FE.32–1982)

49
Kimono, crêpe silk with tie-dyed, applied gold leaf and embroidered decoration
Japan, 1910–30 (V&A: FE.17–1994)

50
Kimono, crêpe silk with freehand paste-resist, applied gold leaf and embroidered decoration
Japan, 1830–80 (V&A: T.266–1968, Given by Lady Palairet in memory of Sir Michael Palairet)

51
Kimono, monochrome figured satin silk with tie-dyed and embroidered decoration
Japan, 1800–50 (V&A: FE.101–1982)

52
Outer kimono, monochrome figured satin silk with tie-dyed and embroidered decoration
Japan, 1800–30 (V&A: FE.28–1984)

53
Outer kimono, monochrome figured satin silk with embroidered decoration
Japan, 1830–80 (V&A: T.269–1960, Mockett Gift)

54
Outer kimono, crêpe silk with freehand paste-resist, painted and embroidered decoration
Japan, 1850–1900 (V&A: T.389–1910)

55
Kimono, crêpe silk with freehand paste-resist, stencilled and embroidered decoration
Japan, 1850–1900 (V&A: T.155–1965, Leach Gift)

56
Kimono, satin silk with embroidered decoration
Japan, 1850–80 (V&A: T.72–1957, Hughes Gift)

57
Outer kimono, crêpe silk with embroidered decoration
Japan, 1868–1912 (V&A: FE.7–1987)

58
Outer kimono, satin silk with embroidered decoration
Japan, 1820–60 (V&A: FE.36–1981)

59
Kimono fabric sample, crêpe silk with freehand paste-resist decoration
Japan, 1937 (V&A: FE.21–1997)

60
Lining of kimono jacket, plain weave silk with painted decoration
Japan, 1930–50 (V&A: FE.148–2002, Given by Moe Co. Ltd)

61
Wedding kimono, crêpe silk with freehand paste-resist and embroidered decoration
Japan, 1934 (V&A: FE.138–2002, Given by Koji Shimojima)

62
Kimono, monochrome figured satin silk with printed decoration
Japan, 1920–40 (V&A: FE.127–1988)

63
Outer kimono, crêpe silk with freehand paste-resist and embroidered decoration
Japan, 1870–80 (V&A: FE.29–1987)

64
Fisherman's festival robe, plain weave cotton with stencil-dyed decoration
Japan, 1900–45 (V&A: FE.102–1982)

65
Kimono, plain weave silk with stencil-printed warp and weft threads
Japan, 1920–50 (V&A: FE.145–2002, Given by Moe Co. Ltd)

66
Child's kimono, plain weave wool with printed decoration
Japan, 1937 (V&A: FE.2–2005)

Further Reading

Gluckman, D. C. and Takeda, S.S.
When Art Became Fashion:
Kosode in Edo period Japan
Los Angeles, 1992

Jackson, Anna
Japanese Country Textiles
London, 1997

Jackson, Anna
Japanese Textiles in the Victoria
and Albert Museum
London, new edition 2008

Japan Textile Colour Design Centre
Textile Designs of Japan, 3 vols
Tokyo and London, 1980

Van Assche, Annie, ed.
Fashioning Kimono:
Art Deco and Modernism in Japan
Milan, 2005

Woodson, Yoko et al.
Four Centuries of Fashion: Classical Kimono
from the Kyoto National Museum
San Francisco, 1997

Digital Images

The patterns reproduced in this book are stored on the accompanying compact disc as jpeg files (at approximately A5-size, 300 dpi). You should be able to open them, and manipulate them, direct from the CD-ROM in most modern image software (on Windows or Mac platforms), and no installation should be required (although we, as publishers, cannot guarantee absolutely that the disk will be accessible for every computer).

Instructions for tracing and tiling the images will be found with the documentation for your software.

The names of the files correspond to the V&A inventory numbers of the images.